BOX OFFICE GOSPEL

Reading Marissa Glover's *Box Office Gospel* feels like having the best kind of conversation with a close friend. Here we can move fluidly between discussing Wonder Woman and Han Solo to current politics and social issues to biblical stories and church attendance because they all tie together in the flow of these poems. We can laugh together, sometimes right after we've discussed something very serious, maybe especially because we've discussed something serious, and we need to laugh. I needed this book.

—Katie Manning, author of *Tasty Other* and
The Gospel of the Bleeding Woman

There's no telling how many times I've purchased a movie ticket just for the joy of sinking into a soft chair in a big, dark room to get away from whatever's going on outside. Many of those times, though, the movies held such power that they brought the real world into sharper focus and altered how I walked back out into it. That's exactly how Marissa Glover's new collection, *Box Office Gospel*, affects me. These poems help us all see the world as it is—with its broken hearts, its tumors, its ugly politics, its war—sometimes from the dark comfort of the theater, sometimes at the elbow of Jon Snow waiting for the White Walkers to arrive. The heroes in Glover's poems might be fictional, but the bullets flying are always real, as is the peril, and as the poet so eloquently states, "We're all just/one conversation away/from breaking." From Bond and John Wick to Deborah, Queen Esther, and other warrior women, each page here offers us the saviors our fragile world needs today. Most importantly, these poems make us know we can be right there with them in the fight. And I can't think of a more valuable gift a poem, or a poet, could give us in these times.

—Jack B. Bedell, author of *Against the Woods' Dark Trunks*,
and Poet Laureate of Louisiana, 2017–2019

Lights, camera, action! Marissa Glover's latest collection brilliantly mixes pop culture with pathos and throws us into a world that only she could craft. Glover gives us something to admire on every page: There's a wish to own a DeLorean so you can travel back in time with the knowledge you have now, plus the words of Winona Ryder as Jo in *Little Women* to reclaim your own power, and then there's the idea of telling a superhot Thor that you don't need his help—that you got this. Simply put: Marissa Glover's *Box Office Gospel* deserve its own star on the Hollywood Walk of Fame.

—Shawn Berman, author *Mr. Funnyman*

BOX OFFICE GOSPEL

Poems

Marissa Glover

MERCER UNIVERSITY PRESS
Macon, Georgia
2023

MUP/ P664

© 2023 by Mercer University Press
Published by Mercer University Press
1501 Mercer University Drive
Macon, Georgia 31207
All rights reserved

27 26 25 24 23   5 4 3 2 1

Books published by Mercer University Press are printed on acid-free paper that meets
the requirements of the American National Standard for Information Sciences—
Permanence of Paper for Printed Library Materials.

Printed and bound in the United States.

This book is set in Adobe Garamond.

Author photograph by Benjamin Watters; photo editing by Stephanie Reed
Photography.

Cover image is a Burgert Brothers 1930 photograph of the Tampa Theatre courtesy Tampa-
Hillsborough County Public Library System.

Cover/jacket design by Burt&Burt.

ISBN   978-0-88146-876-2
LCCN   2023931613
Cataloging-in-Publication Data is available from the Library of Congress

For my son

MERCER UNIVERSITY PRESS

Endowed by

TOM WATSON BROWN
and
THE WATSON-BROWN FOUNDATION, INC.

Contents

NB: For the poems marked with an asterisk, simply aim your smart phone camera at the QR Code printed on the page to hear Marissa Glover deliver her spoken word piece.

What we want
is never simple.

—Linda Pastan, "What We Want"

I.

Pain Is Not Mr. Darcy

We Were Born Sick

And every search
for love is really

just a wish
for medicine.

Every shot
of vodka, poison

antidote for pain.
We cry out

in ecstasy, but
still, we cry.

Each new smile
is a fresh mask

ineffective
for hiding truth:

*It's not the pain
that ruins us—*

*it's what we do
to avoid the pain.*

Some Say the World Will End

As the great cathedral spire collapses—
an avalanche of wood and fire,
remember Jon Snow is not the bastard
everyone thought he was. Remember
the truth of the day before, *before*
you started guessing at the plot,
how it all will end. No one knows

how things begin or end. Things grow
until they don't. Sometimes, we're grateful.
The tumor shrinks—we don't need a reason.
We're glad our eyes can see the trees
take shape again. They are only birch
and maple and pine pocked with ice.
Not White Walkers coming in winter
to kill us while we sleep.

Or the tumor does not shrink.
The spark eats itself full, belches
to twice its size, burns holes
in our prayers. With dragon breath,
doctors whisper a secret heard in a crypt
and carried to the surface. Soon,
everyone will know. Not the origin
or cause—just the epilogue,
a map to where the world is buried.

Look—

The bullet was not meant
for the boy. It was reflex,
retaliation, a warning

of the bad things
a man might do, can do,
will do if you make him

angry enough. The bullet
was meant for the boy's mom—
for being a bad driver, a bad

woman, one who needs
to learn some respect.
Think of the birds

she could have shot with
his kind of ammunition.
But the man missed the mark,

as people full of rage often do.
See the bird on the ground,
slowly picked apart by teeth,

see the flocks gutted and
stuffed for cabin walls,
where they look in flight.

See all the boys whose tummy
hurts, see the moms whose fisted
shirt cannot stop the bleeding.

See all the moms whose tummy
is not bleeding but hurting,
not hurting but empty, not empty

but empty not empty but empty.
Like the shell of a bird
once feathered, once flying

now hollowed with nothing
left but an unseeing socket
in the middle of the street.

How Fast Can You Run?

If we knew two hundred years ago
how fast bullets would travel, how much damage
an ArmaLite could do compared to a musket:
repeating rounds and rounds and rounds and—
would we have signed the same words into law?

If we knew two hundred years ago
how words would bullet soft bodies, the preferred
target of cyber bullies; if we could predict
Trump tweeting his way to POTUS, taking aim
at political opponents and firing—
would we have been more specific about free speech?

If the Flash could travel back in time
without killing Cisco's brother, without erasing
Sara Diggle, without creating aberrations
against everybody's will—would he still run
to save his mom from Zoom?

Not even the Flash is fast enough
to change the past, to rescue the future.
Because if he kept his mom from dying,
he might only be Barry Allen, and then

who would save Central City?

How to Turn Someone in an Interrogation

"He systematically pulled you apart. Piece by
piece, until there was nothing left but pain."
—*Homeland*, Season 2, Episode 5

Rule #1: Look for what
makes them human. Ask
about their ~~mother~~ parent.
Not everyone has
a mother. Find common
ground, shared experiences.
Tell them about your
~~childhood~~ surgery—
stress how hard it was
to recover. Even if their
body has never been cut,
they can imagine.
Show them scars;
they'll know it hurt.
Share enough details
to make it ~~feel~~ real;
invent the rest. After pain,
offer reprieve. Often,
this brief kindness is
all they need to trust.

Rule #2: Be patient.
It will take ~~years~~ time
to find exactly what
you're looking for. After,
exploit the soft spot;

this is the ~~torture~~
vulnerability everyone
wants to avoid. We can't
see it, but we're already
walking around with
numbers over our head,
a red digital countdown
marking the moments left,
like a shot clock telling
us to hurry. Like a timer
on a wired bomb
~~impossible~~ for us to
disarm. We're all just
one conversation away
from ~~breaking~~.

Complicit

My grandpa used to tell me
"Nobody sprouts horns overnight."
And he was right—usually
you can spot the devil a mile away,
if you keep your eyes open.

But we draft the cornerback who runs
real fast because we have a hole
in our defense—never mind that he lost
his scholarship for doing drugs
or beating women. We'll keep going
out with a man who's hot and rich, even
though he sent us unsolicited dick pics.
Post angry memes when it's over,
hold a press conference to play
the fool. But we saw it coming.
We knew.

Decades ago,
Donald Trump sat in his boardroom—
flanked by eager children, surrounded
by suck-ups and cameras, everyone angling
for a job or the money shot—with pursed lips
and finger-pointing "You're fired!"
while the network only heard The O'Jays
singing *moneymoneymoneymoney*
and danced in ratings gold. We watched
contestants and placed our bets, sure
we'd win if we were on the set, nobody caring
what Trump said to Howard Stern or Billy Bush
or what he did to any woman, anywhere.

Jonathan Rhys Meyers Ruined Me for Other Men

On television,
when Henry takes her from behind—
he folds her body into his and holds it
hard against his thighs. His stubble marks
a damask rose upon her cheek.

Her crown slips as his bicep flexes;
his hand commands her neck
to learn the lesson Tudors give.

I wonder if this is how it really happened
when the fat king schtooped his fair lady.

Poor Anne—she dies no matter what,
but now we women find ourselves
aching for a man who was covered in pus-
filled boils and would as soon behead us
as bed us.

#MeToo

Somewhere
Harvey Weinstein is rotting
in a cell, feeling sorry
for himself and blaming women
for all the trouble
his pecker and pride have caused.
Epstein's dead and rotting too.
But what about the movie stars
and mega-rich who keep making
films and money, who knew cats
were being kept in gilded cages
and tortured for their skin—
this fraternity of bystanders,
the Cains who insist they are not
their brother's keeper.

What about David, the Israelite
King, who commanded Tamar
cook food for her brother
and feed him when he was sick
with lust, and then did nothing
for his daughter after Amnon
raped her? Looking the other way
is as old as sin. Just ask Jacob
what he did to defend Dinah.

But somewhere there's a brother
who will not forget his sister,
will not keep quiet. He'll promise
that dog Shechem his sister's hand
if the entire pack of curs convert,

wait until their pecker's sore
from circumcision, then
slaughter them all one by one.
Or he'll invite all the king's sons
to a sheep-shearing party, get 'em drunk
on box wine, find Amnon the rapist
and run him through with a sword.

When He Tells You He's a Bastard, Believe Him

Believe his stories of the past,
the graves dug with eager
shovels, filled to the brim
with bones. Don't dream
of fairy tales, the motherless
girls who marry a prince
and live happily. Leave him
in his reluctance. Let him
stay buried in anger. Remember
Mera, Queen of Xebel,
who spends an entire movie
trying to convince Aquaman
he has what it takes to be a hero.
And Daenerys, Mother of Dragons,
rightful Targaryen Queen,
who loses her throne—and
her life, stabbed in the heart
by the man she tried to make a king.

No More Talk of Violence

Tonight, pick something else.
Don't tell me about Jael, the ibex,
the woman who won a war
with a mallet, driving a tent
peg through General Sisera's
head while he slept. That tale
will not welcome sleep, not when
our land is awash with war,
generals, and too many evil kings.

And not the one about Deborah,
prophetess. The only lady judge
mentioned in the Bible, her name
already buzzes in memory. Besides,
I've had enough of judgment.
So, no more Ruth, no more
sleeping at the foot of a man's
bed, for whatever reason. Women
who follow their man wherever
he goes have their own reward.

Yes, Queen Esther bravely saves
her people by knowing the way
to a man's heart is through his
stomach. Some wives can't cook;
some don't want to. Tell me tonight
of Rahab, the hooker who defies
her country, of Dorcas, the artist
her community cannot live without.
Grant me redemption, resurrection—
a sleep deep enough to dream.

Tell me the story of the girl lit by a
thousand lights, barefoot in miles of
soft green grass unlittered with snakes
or the spurs and sticks that harm, how
she twirls in a trill of fire that does not
consume, cannot be put out, set aflame
by the glittering sparks of chandeliers,
hanging from the dome of heaven.
Tell me this story, then tell me again.

Han Solo on Halloween

I hear his laugh before his knock
and open the door to this mercenary—
hair perfectly mussed, face lit with cheeky grin.

He wants something
but keeps his distance for effect.
His Corellian eyes see right through me, flicker

with recognition. He whispers,
"I like your buns."

But he isn't ready for my tricks or treats,
so I tell him to take his charm next door
because Bria Tharen will give her candy to anyone.

He counters—
calls me Princess Bossy Boots
and makes a show of reaching for his blaster.

We stand in silence,
willing the other to move first.

II.

Brides and Buccaneers

Covert Affairs in Plain Sight

Spoiler Alert:
Auggie and Annie
don't end up together.

I know this
after binge-watching
five years
in a single week.

I thought if I
watched episodes
quickly, skipping
recaps and sleep,
I could fix

what the years
do to romance.
It didn't work

for Mary Shannon
and Marshall Man
either. I tried

with us, too.
Fast-forwarded
through fights;
paused & slow-mo'd
when the sex
was good; rewound
every kind word
you ever said.

The upside
to binging—
it only takes days
to reach the end
when everybody
else waits years
to learn the truth.

Homeland

Sometimes
it helps to think
of the relationship
as a house, a place
where your heart feels
at home until it doesn't.

When it's time to move
on, it helps to remember
Carrie Mathison running
from a hail of bullets
or the truck that's
gunning for her.

Carrie doesn't stall,
doesn't wait around
to see if the driver will
change his mind at the last
second, turn the wheel
or hit the brakes.

Carrie hauls ass.
And if she finds a bomb
hidden in the closet
behind her black jeans
and slinky tank she saves
for manic nights at the bar,
she doesn't stop

to pack a bag. She sprints
downstairs and out the door,
hoping to reach a safe enough
distance before the explosion
knocks her off her feet.

Sometimes, it helps to think
of the relationship as a house
and inside the house is a bomb
and you don't have time
to figure out what's happened
or decide what to take—

there's only time
to save yourself, and barely,
so you leave everything behind
like Carrie does, hair trailing
as she flees.

In her After Action Report,
Carrie is asked to explain
why she left the door open
when she fled, why
she didn't grab her keys.
People assume

she had something to do
with it, was somehow involved
in the plot to blow up her house
or that she won't be able
to stay away, won't know how
to let it go.

Sometimes, it helps to think
of the relationship as a house
and inside the house is a bomb
and there's no need to close
the door on your way out.

Equivocation

You can tell me Trump colluded with the Russians
and nine times out of ten, I'll picture Mikhail
Baryshnikov in black milliskin tights
and tight white shirt, strutting
into secret meetings with his brisés volés
and grands jetés. You can tell me to be serious—
that Putin is a dangerous man, and I'll imagine
Ivan Drago punching Rocky's face to a pulp.
The truth is what we make of it.

My therapist tells me to delete my Twitter.
It's a trigger, each tweet a reminder
of the ways men twist words into weapons.
Trump lies and I catastrophize:
Bridges fall into oceans, I'm flooded
with apocalyptic emotions, memories
of stepping into the ring where conversations
earn glittered belts—bruises, welts—
these heavyweight bouts, his teasing mouth.
The tongue's a trickster.
I swallow balls of cotton until I'm stuffed
like the doll boxed in the closet, her thin lips
an X sewn in red stitches, wedded to silence.

Nothing Gold

When I'm wilted from parenting
and paying bills, when an actor excites me
more than he should, it's easy to imagine
a castle in Sussex or a kilted Jamie Fraser
waiting in Lallybroch to welcome me
as lady of his clan. Somewhere a prince,
somewhere a savior—but these are wisps
of morning gone by noon. Jacobite lairds
don't brush their teeth; every husband has his flaws.

I bet Michal used to love
when David the Giant Slayer danced.
Early on, she would've welcomed his wild moves,
the unchoreographed jubilation after a big win.
And at their wedding reception, both of them
a few drinks in, the King must've cut a rug,
spun his new wife round the room, both of them
high on timbrel and lyre. At first, she's thrilled
to be queen, glad to be back in the palace
after her father Saul lost the kingdom.

But Michal is proof for every wife—*nothing gold
can stay*. One day, you will despise his awkward jig,
feel embarrassed by the joke he's told a thousand times,
wish yourself invisible when he crawls in bed. It's easy
to forget why we married. Pink impatiens yellow quickly
in the Florida sun. We think the rain will be plenty,
but we are always wrong.

Going to the Airport Is Like Going to Church

Most people have been a few times, but no one stays for long.
Not even the faithful, who congregate before going about their business.
At both, money is collected; coffee helps keep folks awake.
Prayers are said for loved ones. People cry tears of joy, or pain.
But it's not a place people stay, not unless they work there. Even then,
they watch the clock—hurry home. We're only there to get somewhere
else.

Press 9 for More Options

On television, Lagertha spends most
of her time traveling from Viking town
to Viking town, from man to man,

plotting to stay alive. History tells us
she's Queen of more than Kattegat,
which isn't even a real place. She's wife

of Ragnar Lodbrok, a man whose name
sounds like a Marvel movie starring
Chris Hemsworth as a superhot Thor.

In the film, evil slaughters the Valkyrie
but Brunnhilde the Asgardian survives
and becomes King when Thor abdicates

the throne. It's nice when the script
offers options. Like when Black Panther
wants to crown Nakia Queen of Wakanda

and nearly chokes when she chooses
her job instead of him. I have options
too: Evacuate before Ragnarök hits, hope

there will be enough gas to last the trip. Or—
stockpile food and water, buy batteries
before the store sells out. Some women pray

the roof will hold; wait for the storm to turn.
Some women strike out on their own,
bolts of lightning from an unforgiving sky.

Built for Letting Go

> "Everything dies, baby, that's a fact;
> but maybe everything that dies
> someday comes back."
> —Bruce Springsteen, "Atlantic City"

The only flat tire I've ever had
I got driving through the parking lot
at Jimmy's Roller Rink—I ran over
a curb looking for your car to see
if you were there, without me,
on a Friday night full of couples'
skates. After Springsteen sang
his angsty ballad, no doubt you
put your left leg in, you put your
left leg out, as the girls in spandex
shook it all about.

The tire wasn't the only thing
to go flat that year. You broke up
with me with a phone call
on Christmas Eve, a call
I had to take in the living room
because that's how land lines
worked. The phone and I, nailed
to the wall—unmovable,
my parents' party guests swirling
around me, a tempest whirling
inside.

If I could find a magic Delorean
with a flux capacitor and tires
that rotate horizontally for upward
thrust, yes, I'd visit the past—but
only to travel with today's strong
arms, built for letting go. And if
everything that dies someday
does comes back, I pray nothing
I've buried returns just as it was.
There's not enough ground to dig
every grave twice.

T'int Right, T'int Fair, T'int Fit, T'int Proper

There's a cliff in Cornwall
where people stand
to look across the sea
toward France. From windy
heights, they throw shells
or pebbles down to water
and make a wish.

Demelza pines for Ross
the way Poldark longs
for lady Elizabeth—
and in the end
we're all Warleggans,
greedily grasping for coins
already tossed to air.

Unanswered desire
burrows deep, makes us
sick with want. The splash
of dreams too faint
to hear. The plucked spring
squill and buttercup will
wither before we reach home.

Instruction Manual for My Future Husband

I was raised on Disney movies, the Princess ones
that always end with a wedding. I don't know
what comes next, but I've been told
it's happily ever after. I'm expecting a prince
who can dance and ride a horse and is good
with a sword. You will disappoint me.

Even if you can dance and ride
a horse and are good with a sword.
Don't despair. Life is full of disappointments.
Try as you might to slay dragons or ogres,
avoid the evil stepmother or wicked witch,
I will cry. You won't know why.

You won't be able to fix me. But you
should still try. I will resent you for trying.
I will tell you I'm not a blender or a car
or one of the kids' toys you can patch up
over the weekend. But I'll resent you
even more if you don't try. So, try.

You can buy flowers. Or chocolate.
Or wine. All of these are nice, and none
of these will work. Vain attempts to scale
a mountain you know nothing about.
The terrain here is dangerous; one wrong step
and off the ledge you go to your death.

You'll wonder if I am worth dying for,
and what your ex is up to these days.
You will be confused and try to recall
everything your mother ever taught you.

You will wish you had a magic wand.
You will want to give up. Don't give up.

Don't waste your energy trying to solve
the troll's riddle so you can pass safely.
There's no safe passage in love. Every
path is a snow bridge. Think of me
as a woman in pieces, a puzzle with no
picture on the box. Start with the edges.

When My Fiancé Says He Wants Us to
Retire in Tennessee

At first, I think it could work.

Growing up, I heard Amy Grant
sing "Another Tender Tennessee
Christmas" with such conviction,
it was easy to believe in love
circling round family like gifts
around the tree. I was filled
with nostalgia for a place I'd
never been, snow I'd never seen.

But early crushes on Bing Crosby
and Fred Astaire lead me to favor
Vermont as the place to call home.
Movies like *White Christmas*
and *Holiday Inn* fill my dreams
with idyllic scenes: treetops glisten,
wearing ice like jewels; the fire inside
crackles and warms. Surely, this
is where love would best take root
and survive the seasons.

Does it really matter where we go?
So far, we've spent every holiday
in sunny Florida, lightning capital
of the country, where we sweat
in the backyard for family
photos, busy swatting away
mosquitos. Our love weathers
each occasion.

In the end, we must be careful
with nostalgia—where we go
in dreams. The tug in our gut
makes us smile and ache, fills us
with desire for love, for home,
for a faraway time, when life
was great. It makes us pine
for places that don't exist
and never did.

You Are the Best Sex You Will Ever Have

One day you will remember him
the way you remember the plot
of certain movies—almost sure
you've already seen it, but not sure
enough to say how the story goes.
You'll think of him in the early dark
before morning, or in the final hours
of autumn before the cold winter falls.

And when your husband has already
left for work, you will return
to him, the first boy you loved,
find him in the soft blush of rising,
half lost in last night's dream, half
aroused by sun's first light. You will
imagine what might have been,
the way it could have happened or would
have happened or should have happened.
This is how memory works.

Time unravels. It's your fingers that count
climax after climax after climax after—
as the clock ticks toward noon.
It's not birdsong that has you humming
over the stove at dinner. But it's no man
either. So tell the specters that come
in dreams, the distant echoes at dawn,
it's your body you are touching. This sweat,
this love, is of your own making.

III.

Enchanted

James Bond, Mitch Rapp, and John Wick
Walk into a Bar

Color doesn't matter: It can happen to Idris Elba as DCI John Luther
or Michael B. Jordan as Tom Clancy's John Clark. It's a man thing.

So many women have lost their lives to fridging, the plot device
that kills off a hero's love interest to compel him to act,

that it's hard for us to avoid penis envy. Who wants to die
so that a man finds his path, answers his destiny to rid the world

of evil, one villain at a time? But if every man is an island, make me
Santorini, Palawan, or Doorn. Give me Q's cool gadgets and fast

expensive cars. Watch me drive over the cliff and survive, sexier
for the scars—bloodied by cuts from punches that land like

mosquitos on a body hardened like Hercules. Call me Adonis,
Apollo; let me live, a god, forever. Just don't misunderstand

and make me a boy. Not Huckleberry Finn, not Peter Pan. Not
Harry Potter, Peeta, or Lloyd Dobler—no teenagers. What happens

when they grow up? Make me a man, like the ones in movies,
the ones who always get it right, even when they get it wrong.

I Wish I Were Mississippi State in the
Bottom of the Ninth

Because a higher seed in a tournament is like having a PhD: it gets you tenure and cushy committees, gets you into bars without paying a cover charge, discounts at the Lexus dealer. This is the kind of clout people sell their soul to snort, ride that high even higher, but top seeds are meant to be knocked out in early rounds. Because Texas is already big enough. Because I don't like the color orange. Because I'd rather be Cinderella than Icarus. Because I want a taste of success—not a bite big enough to choke on—just a pinch nestled between lip and teeth, something to spit when I'm angry, when I'm nervous, when I'm ready to fuck you up. Because I'm an underdog and can sniff out other underdogs, and we run in packs through your posh neighborhood. Because somebody has to win and why not the boys from M—I—Crooked Letter—Crooked Letter —I—Crooked Letter—Crooked Letter—I—Humpback—Humpback —I. Because I want to shock the world with a walk-off single to center, because I want a shot at the series final, because I want to be more than anyone ever thought possible. Because when people say my name, I want it to be with envy—part prayer, part praise. Because I want people to know my name. Know it. Say it. Never forget it.

Beware the Sister

Joseph thought he had it bad
when his ten brothers plotted to kill him
for dreaming he was better than them.
To be fair, it wasn't just the visions—
I'll be a big star in the sky and your lesser lights
will bow down to my super shiny one—
that ticked everyone off. No,
Joseph had to go on and on about it.

Teenagers are like that—
they dream they will grow up and do great things,
and at seventeen they are foolish enough
to think everyone wants to hear the details.
Nobody likes a show-off,
wearing Daddy's flashy colored coat
when it's a hundred degrees outside.

Still, Reuben knew better than to murder Joseph.
The oldest, he'd had years of practice—
pulling brother off brother, knowing when to step in
between punches and say *Enough*
so no one needed stitches. But Judah suggests slavery
and the brothers take a vote, selling shiny-star Joseph
to the Ishmaelites for twenty shekels of silver.

Believe it or not, this is a poor man's pittance
compared to the money Meghan Markle's sister makes
selling "Princess Pushy" stories to the press.
There's a reason the movie is called *Mean Girls*.
Boys will kick you in the nuts or throw you down a well,
but you will always see it coming. Imagine how
Lee Radziwill felt when Jackie stole Aristotle.

Look at poor Kate Spade—not even in the ground
before her estranged sister sinks the knife.

Beware the sister who holds your head underwater
a little too long in the pool playing shoulder wars.
Beware the sister who returns your favorite doll
one eye missing, makes out with your boyfriend on a dare.
Beware the sister who was born before you
and whose flower fades as yours blooms.
Beware the sister. Beware.

Where Have All the Children Gone?

When I hear the wailing travel down the tracks—an echo of Piggy's conch blowing across the beach, this monster stealing through the graveyard, grinding through the dead—I think of Mowgli, the boy who ran wild in *The Jungle Book* half-naked, covered only by a loincloth and liberty. Half-brave, you and I climb the trestle. The metal is cold and not to be trusted, a drunk swaying side to side in the dark. Seniors in college, we throw our shoes and clothes onto the railroad but refuse to follow through with jumping. We aren't ready for much of anything.

Helen, whose face could launch a thousand ships, would go skinny-dipping. I stay on shore, swimming in rum. Maybe drinks help us come to terms with our mediocrity, give us courage to flaunt our abundant curves or obvious lack—if only to ghosts. We joke about heeding the call of nature and not wanting to piss on the dead. We watch our steps, tripping through wet grass slick with mist, as if dodging land mines.

We talk about Achilles and the beauty of an imperfect body. We are not gods, and our shame at stripping keeps us moving from shadow to shadow, hating the brief moments the moon proves us human. Walking up a dandelion hill, past stone markers too small for grown-ups, I ask, "Where have all the children gone?" You keep walking. But it's us, I think. Naked at the edge of adulthood one last time, we make sure we're hidden by something and then we make our peace.

The Bible Doesn't Tell Us

how Eve found out about the murder—
Was she near the field, milking goats
maybe, close enough to hear the scuffle?
Did Adam break the news that night
when he got home from work? Was it gossip,
spread through the community like leprosy?

After, the camera follows Cain
when it should cut to Eve, a close-up
on the first mother grieving both her sons—
forever lost to her over an offering.
If God could hear Abel's blood
crying from the earth, imagine
the cries Eve must have heard.
Imagine her praising both the fruit
and the flesh, telling the boys how much
she loved them, how special they were.

In the beginning, there was fratricide—
Romulus and Remus; Cambyses kills Bardiya.
Jealousy, a power grab, anger
over who pleased the Lord—the impetus
doesn't matter; sin still crouches at the door.
Claudius kills Hamlet; Michael kills
Fredo; Scar kills Mufasa. Geta dies
in his mother's arms.

Mothers need to know how to mourn the dead
and how to mourn the living. How to let Adam
back into bed—how to birth Seth and start again.
We pray for guidance. We open the Good Book
but nothing's there. It's all too much for God to say.

Searching for Sanctuary

I.

In the Old Testament, God
told Moses to set aside cities,
places where persecuted
people could find safety,
a refuge in Canaan
after the terror of Egypt.
This right of asylum
in countries, or cities,
or churches has always been
for the outcast—accidental criminals,
runaway slaves, the righteous,
people looking for better
life, somewhere
gangs and government
aren't trying to kill them.
Even in America today, folks
still sit on the frithstool, waiting
for shelter and sanctuary.
Most of us are too busy
watching Netflix to notice.

II.

Some scholars see Luke Cage
as a Christ figure, rising
from the water tank torture
in Seagate Prison, breaking
the chains of sin and death,
beating hell and the grave,
ascending to the heights
of Harlem, omnipotent.

But Luke Cage isn't God.
He's anointed at baptism,
raised to new life, imbued
with power. But he's a man
on a mission—a superhero,
trying to seek and save
that which is lost.

      III.
He first reaches Harlem's
Paradise, an anti-sanctuary
doubling as the villains' lair,
where he is soon cast out—
banished from this fallen Eden.
Luke tries church next. His father's
the pastor. Surely, the saints
will warmly welcome him
since the sinners didn't. Sweet
Christmas! Luke learns
there's a hypocrite in the pulpit.
For a moment, Luke finds peace
at Pop's Barbershop. This sacred space
where Black men gather for cuts
and contact, where they can
be safe—free to shoot
the shit, talk smack, question
Pop's decision to put Pat Riley
on the list for free haircuts.
Here, the grown teach the young;
the wise show the fools: *What is
hard work? What does it take
to be a man?*

IV.
Luke Cage almost found sanctuary
at the barbershop. Then evil
broke in and shot up the place.
And so it will be in the last days
when pestilence again haunts
the earth—truth and doctors will die;
the government will shut
everything down. Everything
but anger, conspiracies, and death.
When the old and the ill are persecuted
in great number, when allies are attacked,
when color is again more likely to suffer,
when southern stylists defy the law
to keep cutting clients' hair, don't believe
the posters people hold to the sky.
No matter how dark or deep the red
and blue words on their lily-white
signs, none of these barbershops
in the news will be manned by heroes.

Sinner's Prayer

God, grant me the resilience
of a wild squirrel who steals seed
from the squirrel-proof bird feeder,
hanging upside down on a wire
by only his toes as both hands shovel
food to mouth. Give me the audacity
of the sandhill crane stopping four
lanes of traffic, sauntering from golf
course to neighborhood, where he pecks
the parked car until the paint chips.

God, grant me the energy of ants
invading my kitchen, the endless work
of a thousand female bodies, constant
movement, as they avoid traps I've set
by the stove, on the floor at every door,
and in the shower where the caravans
don't stop their exercise from drain
to window from window to drain—
even while I'm washing—two lines
of perpetual motion nothing can exhaust.

Speaking of exhausted, God,
give me the patience of Mary,
mother of Jesus—the teenage boy
who intentionally got lost on family
vacation and wouldn't give his mom
a straight answer when she asked
why he would do such a thing. Yes,
make me patient like Mary, who managed
not to knock her son into the middle
of next week. Sweet Baby Jesus,

grant me the confidence of a middle-aged
man who read half a Wikipedia article or
watched a video on YouTube and is now
preaching on Facebook, screeching
about free speech and wondering
why his posts keep getting flagged.
Make me as certain as he who knows
more than the rest of us—mere sheep
to the slaughter, we who are not hell-
bent but already burning.

Casting the Amygdala and Hippocampus
as Monsters in the Attic

> "This is called a 'neuralyzer'....The red eye here isolates
> and measures the electronic impulses in your brains.
> More specifically, the ones for memory."
> —Agent K, *Men in Black*

It's different when Spider-Man decides
to let Dr. Strange cast the spell
that will wipe Peter Parker
from memory. The hero chooses
the multiverse over himself.
This is not the same as Agents K and J,
galaxy defenders, who don't ask
permission to erase people's
minds with the flashy-thing.

In November when the ground
is wet, I drive by the house
where Sadie died. The new
owners made the carport
a garage, painted the white brick
yellow. Is the picnic table
my grandfather built still out back,
does the fence still hide a grove?
Do neighbors hear growls at night?

If there were such things
as superheroes, it's an easy choice,
really. Most people would pick
the neuralyzer instead of the spell.
Tell me—what sorrow still visits you?
What unexpected freeze-frame,

a gut punch from the past? No,
we want to be remembered. But
there's so much we'd like to forget.

It's Always Hard to Get out of Bed

the morning after a school shooting.
On the drive, the thirteen-year-old asks
why there are so many love bugs, why they kill
themselves on the windshield. He feels sorry
for the one just along for the ride, who never
sees what's coming. The ten-year-old wants
to know what she can put down to stop
Wall Breakers if she doesn't have a Skeleton
Army. In Clash Royale, players have options.
I wonder if I'll be able to wash off the bug
splatter before the acid eats away the paint.
I wonder what kind of mistake we make,
becoming mothers.

We feel like drivers for Uber Eats, delivering
children for the day to consume. We watch band
kids lug to class, newly suspicious. Yesterday,
the shooter hid his guns in a guitar case.
Judgement Day—a boy runs down halls, fleeing
the danger his mother warned him about.
But the Terminator protects John Connor
from Cyberdyne's T-1000. Schwarzenegger's
shotgun blooms from a box of roses. We pray
none of it's real—it's all special effects for ratings,
CGI or squib rigs. We pray for a Guardian, just in case
everything's real—make sure our kids aren't felled
by bullets or liquid metal arm-swords that pin people
to the wall like bugs.

And the Oscar Goes to—

Don't believe the actors when they complain about the price of fame and say they hate it—the bright lights, the constant click of paparazzi bulbs, being hounded round the clock—it's what they've been dreaming of since winning the lead in their middle school play, since they dropped out of college and moved to L.A., where they wait tables and practice how to stand at just the right angle, how to smile, pretending a question about the menu is a red carpet interview. Don't believe them when they cry on stage at the Oscars and *omigosh!* they had no idea and have nothing prepared and then they recite the most perfectly imperfect speech—the one they practiced in the bathroom mirror, holding a hairbrush.

When Brad Pitt as Benjamin Button grows too young to be with Daisy, I don't cry as he dies in her arms—because he dies for a gambling debt in *A River Runs Through It;* gets mauled to death by a bear in *Legends of the Fall;* he's hit by a car in *Meet Joe Black.* And I can't hate Christian Bale as Dick Cheney because I still love him as Laurie in *Little Women,* even though he didn't adore Jo the way he said he did or he wouldn't have fallen for Amy. You want to know who deserves an award for playing their part, for making it believable? Mothers.

Applaud the woman who had no idea it would be this hard, pretending to pay attention to a toddler's story of the red truck beeping his horn he beeped his horn did you hear the red truck beep did you see the truck did you hear the horn beepbeepbeep went the horn in the red truck. The woman gives her daughter the car keys when she'd rather hand her a gun, or pepper spray, or *anything* to protect her while she's out on a date. Instead, she pays for AAA, waves, and acts like she's okay. She hides her fear and saves her tears for the shower, where water washes it all away—before the curtain opens again: The woman is in bed with a husband she's forgotten; she quickly gets into character and delivers her lines.

In the Beginning

The curse is like the creation.

Events repeat. The action builds,
culminating in a strange cycle of life,
then death.

On the first day there is bloating.
On the second day there is blood.
On the third day there are mood swings.
On the fourth day there is blood.
On the fifth day there are cramps.
On the sixth day there is blood.
Always, the promise of pain.

The seventh day is set aside as a day of
bingeing. But grease and caffeine
only make it worse, another punishment
for eating what we shouldn't have.

IV.

After Sodium Thiopental

The Archaeology of Dryer Lint

This morning I found something important
in the lint screen of my drying machine,
but I don't know for sure what I've lost. It's not
the Ark of the Covenant or a mysterious stone
to rescue children. The tiny balls of shriveled

paper could be anything—work's 1040 for
the year's taxes, my mom's pound cake recipe
I asked for last time I visited, an idea
for a poem that would've won awards—
and there's no one here to help figure it out.

No Indiana Jones with fedora and bullwhip
and dry-clean only leather jacket; no one
to excavate, fit the pieces together, match
jagged edge to crooked corner. Even in
my ignorance, I'm sure I've lost more

than I've found—these easy quarters
that roll and bang the drum on occasion,
each coin a small, rare gift. Maybe there's
no reason now to mourn; maybe it's only
a tissue once knotted with phlegm.

But maybe it was a map to where
this life will go, something charted
with predictions I could learn to read,
something telling me how to prepare,
how to be ready.

What's in a Name

Our name is the first secret we tell a stranger.

I know from Sunday school
that Father Abraham had many sons
and that God changed his name from Abram
to *Father of Many Nations* as part of the promise.

It was like smack talk—same as Deion Sanders
showing up to play ball; here you call him
Prime Time. Even before the pro contracts
and Super Bowl rings—he is he that he says he is
and woe to the Gators and Tigers who do not believe.
"Danny Rand" won't pack the punch of "Iron Fist."
Don Diego de la Vega is a cowardly fop.
No one's afraid of Bruce Banner.

After the name change, Big Abe could roll up
to Canaan, or wherever, with his flock and barren wife—
a walking talking billboard, calling things that be not
as though they be. His introductions functioned
as prophecy: *Hello, I'm the Father of sand and stars and sons.*
Seems the name mattered. Even for God,
the promise was not enough.

My father promised my mother they'd name all the kids
with the letter "M." My brother Michael's babysitter
was called Larissa—a pretty name, my parents agreed.
So I was born Marissa & some websites say the name's
from Mara, meaning *bitter*, or Mary, *of the sea.*
It's hard to tell, really.

After the divorce, my dad broke his promise,
naming his third & final child Joshua—
the brother who watched *Inspector Gadget*
and *G.I. Joe* with me; the one who played cowboy,
galloping through palmettos, cap guns blazing
in the sun; a boy who was, and is, God's way
of saving all who need saving.

None of My Childhood Heroes Prepared Me for This

My teenager asks me how long zits last, and I tell him about washcloths and exfoliating soap and his father's acne scars because I grew up on G.I. Joe and knowing is half the battle. It's not the answer he wants. Mine never are. Like when he asks if he can go to the pool with the boys—and I remember fourteen, the dive, my ambulance ride. So I let him shoot hoops, hoping it will be enough. Hoping he remembers Billy Blazes and Wendy Waters and to think like a rescue hero, think safe.

When he asks how much longer we have to do this—wash hands, wear masks, go to school online, I smartly report CDC guidelines and the governor's timelines and keep right on rattling about how the pantry's stocked with soup and crackers, just in case, and thermometers and extra inhalers and his favorite sports drink, the one with all the electrolytes. Oh, and only acetaminophen because research says it's better for this kind of inflammation than ibuprofen. None of this brings him comfort.

He has stopped listening. Something about a rainbow and a siege and the number six. "We've got this," I tell him again, like I'm Hannibal and this is war and my son's part of the A-Team. I've always loved it when a plan comes together. But none of my childhood heroes help me now. None of the old wisdom works. Yet here I am, trying to McGyver away his pain, McGyver a way for us to recoup such loss, when I can't even Go Go Gadget myself any taller to once more perfectly hug the boy who has outgrown me.

Self-Concept

Passing a security checkpoint
to board a plane, I am asked
to identify all the names
I recognize on the screen.
My knowledge of connections
will prove I am the real
Marissa Glover. One name
is my ex-husband's new wife.

In a single moment, I consider
denying the connection, as if
not highlighting her name
could erase her. Make me
wife again. Change me
into someone I recognize.

When I get home, I google
"Marissa Glover" and see
all the different roads I have
walked. Frost didn't know
about search engines when he
said we are just one traveler.
I am an Operations Manager,
a basketball player, a Professor of
Cell and Developmental Biology.

The next time I fly, I remember
Winona Ryder as Jo in *Little Women*.
When the man seated next to me
tells me what I should have been
instead of a poet, I can only reply,
"I should have been a great many things."

I Am Not Uncertain

Wonder Woman needs an invisible plane
because she's stunning—a goddess.
High-cut bikini bottoms highlight
strong Amazonian thighs. Long legs
laced in knee-high boots, a kind of kink,
were made for kicking ass. And the tight
red corset fringed with gold barely contains
her large perfectly perky breasts—
the emblazoned eagle a beacon of something
other than freedom. This Diana Prince
is most men's fantasy. She can stop traffic,
and wars, dressed like this. On Themyscira,
her sisters let her live in peace. But here,
with us, she needs the jet to get around safely,
undetected. Or she just needs to age a little.
Let Wonder Woman reach fifty, sixty, and
no one will see her no matter what she wears.
Old age is a woman's superpower, if only
it felt like one.

Using Elixir Efficiently Is the Key to Victory

Balloons are like New Year's resolutions,
an unwise investment—all of them
unlikely to last very long. No matter
what we do, they leak helium
and sink slowly to the ground.

Then there are the balloons that got
stuck in the tall oak at the park
near our house, the ones I bought
for the Pacifier Party I threw for my son
at eighteen months. Back when I was ready
for him to grow up, back when he loved
balloons and cheerfully waved goodbye
to them, squealing in delight to see them
rise toward the sky, not realizing all
that he was letting go.

He howled terribly that night,
unable to soothe himself to sleep.
I got on my hands and knees, then,
praying to find some forgotten binky—
fallen, lost, between my child's crib
and the wall.

At eight, after a long day of school,
my son glances up from his video game
and asks, "Why didn't Achilles' mom
just hold him by a spot that was already
protected and dip him again
to cover his heel? The way she did it
was dumb. No wonder he died."

If there were immortal words,
vows we could make and not break,
I'd tell him, "Any mom would do
so many things differently
given the chance." I'd teach him
chances are like balloons.

Mary, Did You Know?

Yes, she knew,
as all moms know—
the instant letdown
of milk at his cry,
the look in brown eyes
that says he feels pain,
his smell after a long day
chiseling and stacking
stones, catching barbels
or musht.

She knew all
that other stuff too.
An angel told her,
remember?
Appeared to her,
said she'd soon be pregnant,
and Joseph was not
the father.
The prophets warned
what would happen next.

I'm more curious
about what Mary *didn't* know,
what no mom knows,
what's impossible
to know.
Like how quickly
his feet would be the size
of hammers, how soon
he'd choose his own path.

Or how much
it would hurt
to watch him
suffer, how hard
it would be
to feel the blood
urge for revenge
and take none.

How Many Tears Can a Woman Cry
Before She Has No Tears Left?

This is a trick question.
Like, "If a rooster laid an egg
on the top of a roof, which way
would the egg roll?" Or, "How many
animals did Moses take on the ark?"

There is no right answer
because the question itself
is wrong. How can we number
the sum of a woman's tears
if she never stops crying?

Psalm 56:8 says God stores
our tears in a bottle. It must be
a bottle the size of a planet,
a universe, a gigantic black hole.
This is a metaphor, of course.

There is no bottle that big.
Maybe there is no bottle at all.
Maybe God is a poet and this
is His way of saying he sees
our pain, that our tears matter—

that despite being countless,
each one counts for something.
God keeps track of our sorrows,
writes them down in a book.
This is how we know for sure

God is a poet—with his metaphors
and his bottle of tears and his book
of sorrows. We know He somehow
sees fit to save our tears instead of
dry them. We just don't know why.

How Foolish It Is to Burn with Want

Riders aren't scored if they fall off the bull under eight seconds; the fools who last long enough still aren't guaranteed to win. In numerology, eight is the mathematical symbol for anything that can be foreseen. It looks like infinity. In Chinese culture, eight is the luckiest number, giving people intuition and insight. It sounds like the word for making money. The Eighth Amendment prohibits the federal government from imposing excessive fines or bail, protects citizens from cruel and unusual punishment. My neighbor swears she didn't know her son was growing pot in his room until his lamps burned the whole house down. An eighth is a common measurement of marijuana, enough to roll some blunts or a handful of joints. Seekers look for peace in gardens among agapanthus but it takes a lifetime to travel the eightfold path. By the time we see new light, it is already old. My son is barely eight when he decides he's too big to be held. "Let go," he says, his rib cage hollowed and cold. No one needs a Magic 8 Ball to know how foolish it is to burn with want, how unlucky it'd be to have all the answers.

We Will Never Be Gods

In school, we're taught the soft spot—
expected to find comfort in Achilles' heel
or Superman's kryptonite. *They're just like us*

we imagine, rejoicing in their weakness, willing
Lex Luthor or Paris of Troy to discover the truth
we already know, prove the hero human.

But Achilles doesn't die from an arrow;
he's still living now, here, thousands of years
after the war has ended. And Superman

doesn't stay buried, no matter what the Batman
movie says. Gods and Superheroes always find a way
to resurrection. Don't kid yourself—

Doomsday is the fate of humans. We are mortal
to the end, if not because of our planet or parents
then because our weakness is hubris, the fatal flaw

buried deep in our heart. We secretly wish the hero
to die, cheer when the greatest among us stumbles.
Glued to the news—when the golden boy loses his luster

we take comfort, dancing in our own dull glow.

The Lord Speaks in Metaphor

I've never felt comfortable arguing with Jesus.
(It's not easy, disagreeing with God.)
He says all it takes to move mountains is faith
the size of mustard seeds—Matthew 21:21; 17:20.
Move, mountain, move. Be cast into the sea.

Mountains don't move for me.

When I was little,
I'd pretend I was Wonder Woman.
I practiced transformation:
arms out, half turn to the left, spinning
round and round and round, hoping
for a flash of light.

Mine is not a magic belt. These bracelets
don't deflect bullets. And if I had a golden lasso
that made people tell the truth—well,
God knows I'd have roped half the world by now.

But I'll confess: I've always been more
Viking Shield Maiden than superhero.
I'm Lagertha—unruly woman, wild hair, dirty hands.
My head's too big for a tiara, my thighs too wide
for a blue bikini with stars. I struggle with miracles.
Sometimes, I don't even know how to pray.

I'll cook chicken and stars soup from a can,
scratch my son's back until he sleeps, counting
moles like rosary beads, stay awake all night.
And in the morning, every morning, I rise.

One foot in front of the other isn't glorious,
but the mountains I cannot move—

I climb.

Acknowledgments

Mr. Darcy is a beloved character played by Colin Firth in the BBC's film adaptation of Jane Austen's *Pride and Prejudice*.

The poem title "We Were Born Sick" was inspired by countless sermons and Hozier's song "Take Me to Church." The final sentence in the poem is taken from dialogue in *The Letter for the King*, a television series developed by Will Davies for Netflix and inspired by Tonke Dragt's 1962 novel *De brief voor de Koning*.

"Some Say the World Will End" was inspired by the fire that destroyed part of the Notre Dame Cathedral, an event that transpired the day after a shocking episode of HBO's hit series *Game of Thrones*. The poem title is borrowed from Robert Frost's poem "Fire and Ice," which debates what will happen to us—and why. The phrase "dome of heaven" in the poem "No More Talk of Violence" is a hat tip to Robert Frost and his poem "Birches," which might be the world's most perfect poem and will forever be a favorite of mine. The poem title "Nothing Gold" and the line "nothing gold can stay" is lifted from Robert Frost's poem "Nothing Gold Can Stay."

The phrase "every breaking wave" in the poem "Brides and Buccaneers" is a hat tip to Bono and U2.

The phrase "T'int Right, T'int Fair, T'int Fit, T'int Proper" is often repeated in the BBC television show *Poldark*.

The poem title "I Am Not Uncertain" is a line used by financial traders on the Showtime series *Billions*.

The poem title "Using Elixir Efficiently Is the Key to Victory" is a phrase seen in the video game app Clash Royale as advice to players on how to succeed. The most devastating message a player can see flash across on their cell phone screen during a game is "Your teammate has left the match."

In psychology, "self-concept" is the mental perception we have of ourselves, embodying the answer to the question *Who am I?* It's developed, in part, by our interactions with others.

The title and idea behind the poem "Mary, Did You Know?" responds to the popular Christmas song co-written by Mark Lowry and Buddy Greene.

Special thanks to the editors and publications in where many of these poems first appeared, sometimes under a different title or in a different form: *Autumn Sky Poetry Daily, Be Kind Rewind Anthology, CP Quarterly, Drunk Monkeys, Emerge Literary Journal, FEED Lit Mag, Fresh Air Poetry, Ghost City Review, Gyroscope Review, Isacoustic, Louisiana Literature, Marvelous Verses Anthology, Mineral Lit Magazine, miniskirt magazine, Minyan Magazine, MORIA Literary Magazine, Muddy River Poetry Review, ONE ART: A Journal of Poetry, Paddler Press, Rat's Ass Review, Rattle, River Mouth Review, Schuylkill Valley Journal, Sky Island Journal, Stoneboat Literary Journal, SWWIM Every Day, The Adriatic, The Cabinet of Heed, The Daily Drunk, The Furious Gazelle, The Lumiere Review, The Mythic Circle, The Opiate, The Westchester Review, Three Drops from a Cauldron, Vamp Cat.*

Another special thanks to Jack Bedell, Katie Manning, Shawn Berman, and Keith O'Shaughnessy. These generous humans—each a writer I admire—gladly read this manuscript before it was a book and blessed it with their praise.

I'm grateful for my publisher, Marc Jolley, and his patient team of Bears at Mercer University Press. They make me and my words look better than we are.

Stephen Parrish graciously reads my emails and random questions and has consistently said the right thing at the right time to help me keep going.

My family, friends, and colleagues are kind enough to buy my books, read my poems, and say nice things about them. This means more to me than they know.

My husband doesn't always understand my poems, but he understands that I'm a poet—that's the greater gift, and I love him for it (and for a million other things).

Son, I pray you grow to know and speak and live the truth; to use your powers for good; and to always act justly, love mercy, and walk humbly with your God. I love you forever.

About the Author

Marissa Glover earned her Bachelor of Arts degree at Mercer University in 1996, where she double-majored in English and Philosophy and played on the tennis team. While at Mercer, she was privileged to study under Will D. Campbell, Dana Gioia, Adrienne Bond, and Linda Pastan and to be taught by the irreplaceable Papa Joe and Terrible Trim.

Marissa received her master's in English literature and a graduate certificate in creative writing from the University of South Florida in 2012 and now works as a learning design coach and literacy specialist. Before academia, she worked as a writer and editor for various companies for more than fifteen years.

A Florida native, Marissa spends most of her time sweating and swatting bugs. Her writing has been widely published in various journals and anthologies, but her best work will always be on her parents' refrigerator.

Marissa's first book of poetry, *Let Go of the Hands You Hold*, was published by Mercer University Press in 2021. This is Marissa's second collection of poems.